A Rudimentary of Art

Anthony Dover

Impressionism

When Cezanne started on his walk to Mt.St.Victoire every day to paint it,the locals in Aix on Provence called it Cezanne hour.He did the same every morning and evening.
The artist this book is about was given encouragement after the first painting he did.After getting what he desired,a reason to live,he painted his first painting, a sunset.
Then to begin his artistic journey he trudged up the hill in his town to get to the local library and to borrow books on impressionism. The heaviness of the first few steps in art gave him backache and as he went his house the locals began talking.
The impressionist movement was really the beginning of the modern world and although it was said they were preserving their world it was at time of change with the industrial revolution.Nevertheless they seem to be both a beginning and an end.A signpost,the paintings being painted quickly; Of scenes that were disappearing.
Studying the impressionist way and painting by reading the borrowed books the artist learns placement of colour,a myriad of different strokes which combine in an almost pattern of light and shade.
The exactness or random way of painting can never be understood by a first glance what the good impressionist meant.
He stands facing down the day which becomes the canvas

and attuned and personal the closeness of the artists eye to the picture is revealed.
Whether it is quickly envisioned and done at such a speed with the belief that it will become the imagined when viewed from a distance.
Close inspection of a piece reveals so called careless strokes or errors which in retrospect seem to be qualified by the later brushstrokes.Is then impressionism merely a starting point For painters as it forces the belief in trial and error in perfectionism,then the imaginary and then hope.Often a novice painter finds hope in impressionist art as it offers a friendly introduction to painting.

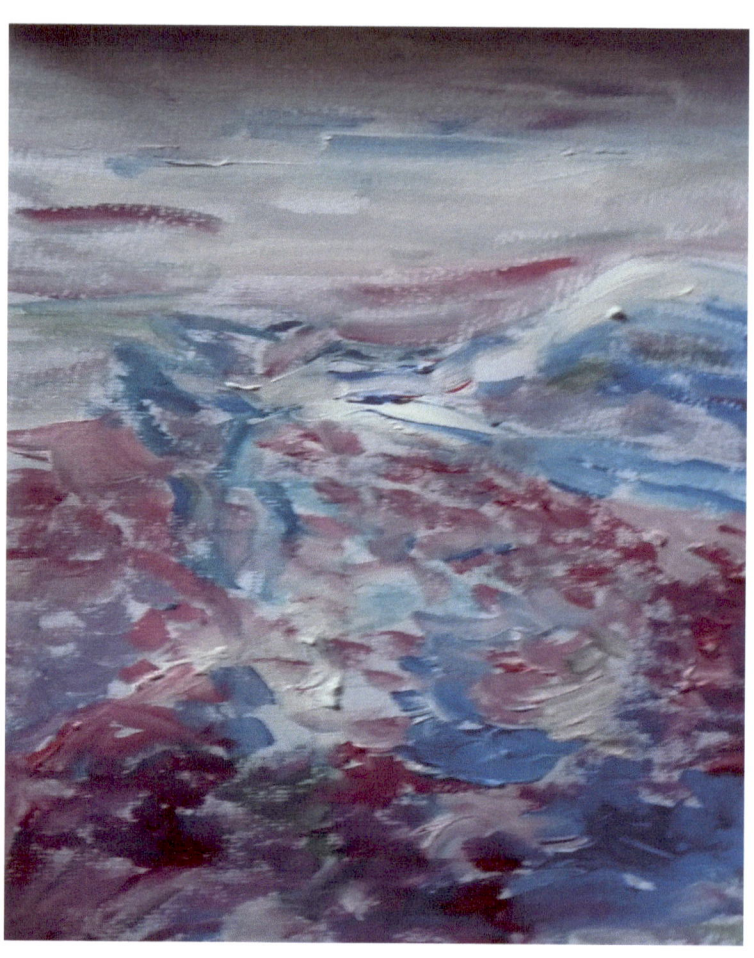

Post impressionism

As far as the impressionism goes and as the brushstrokes suggest realities in the dreams it creates.It is a fleeting glance of life.With post-impressionism it is often lineated by an outline or an edge which whilst still suggesting it gives guidance on how to perceive life in the later in the latter years of the nineteenth century.The block of coloured lines defining the subject help to astonish the viewer of its importance.This is really the essence of great art and because a real post=impressionist is rare and although several artists have been called pariahs like Cezanne and Van Gogh the real ones often weren't recorded.The works which were vastly beautiful were secreted away.Russian post-impressionist are the best but finding them on the internet is difficult.

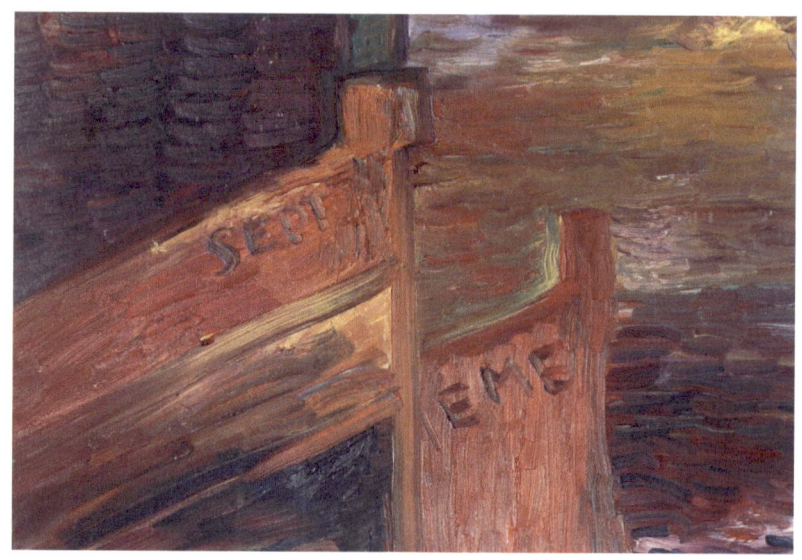

Expressionism

Express;express what? Your emotions.Your feelings. Mostly with conflicting colours juxtaposition of form with space to interact.Firstly between painter and canvas and then canvas with viewer in an emotional exchange often at the moment of rapture,bringing tears.There were several artists who pioneered this in an attempt to communicate with colour,to spread a message of humanity.Often the actual paintings weren't that skillfull but really like an outburst in a realisation captured forever.If fireworks are exciting for children,expressionism is for adults.Like most art which is considered normal for the untutored it still became a recognised theme or movement.

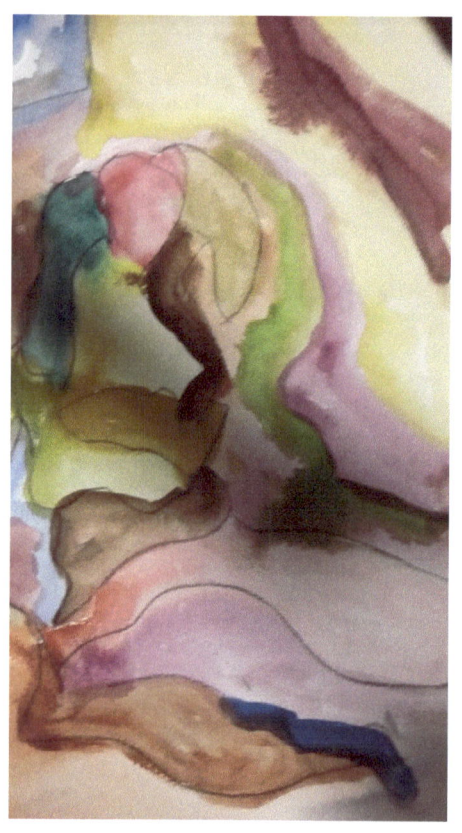

Myriadism

Myriadism is any style of work but one which has many different meanings. This was phrased during the early 21st century as people tried to escape from being categorised And tried to subvert the centuries' lost and meek obedience to it. Many different meanings suggest freedom and intelligence. Although surrealism nearly came to this, it stopped short of this rather stealing rather than giving.
The point of myriadism is to stimulate thought. It helps people to see more in life and like a child's possession enables learning.

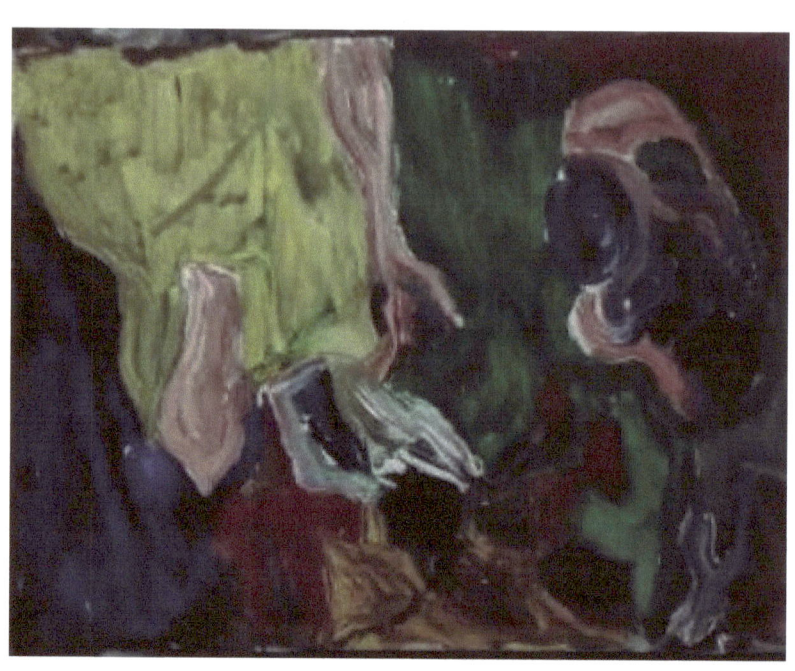

AD09s

These were born of an apocalypse, the rushing landscapes,the haunted nowhere lands and the mystical feel to them.They were called the monika AD to be signifying the year Anno Domino and as after the turn of the millenium the numbers were counted.This is because many people around that time believed Christ had come again and that time had been set back to the start.These lands and places were revealed as the fire stormed in the clouds,the earth shook and the artist revcording it with a quick pen and an even quicker brush.Although destruction and after the beauty which is pictured is haunting they remain rare as the scenes were only witnessed then.

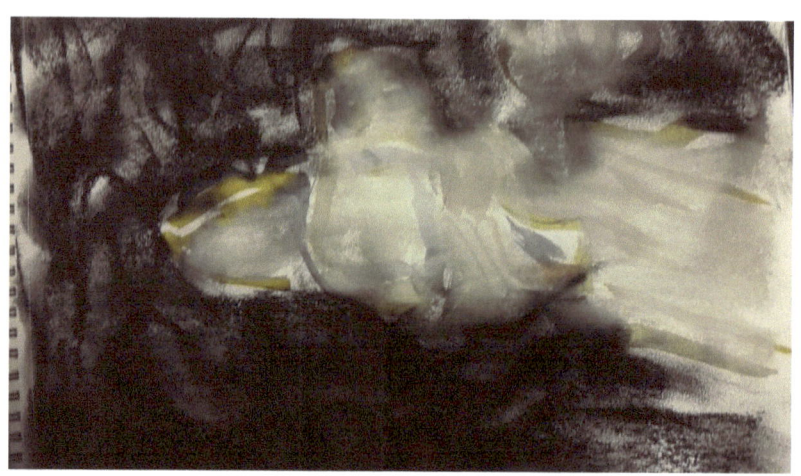

Van Goghism

The belief that Van Gogh was someone of great importance has been around for sometime. These are thousands of theories as to why. Perhaps he was a messiah, an alien because some of his landscapes are or a saint. Belief in him as a pariah an open door to the 20th century is also apparent. No more needs to be said.

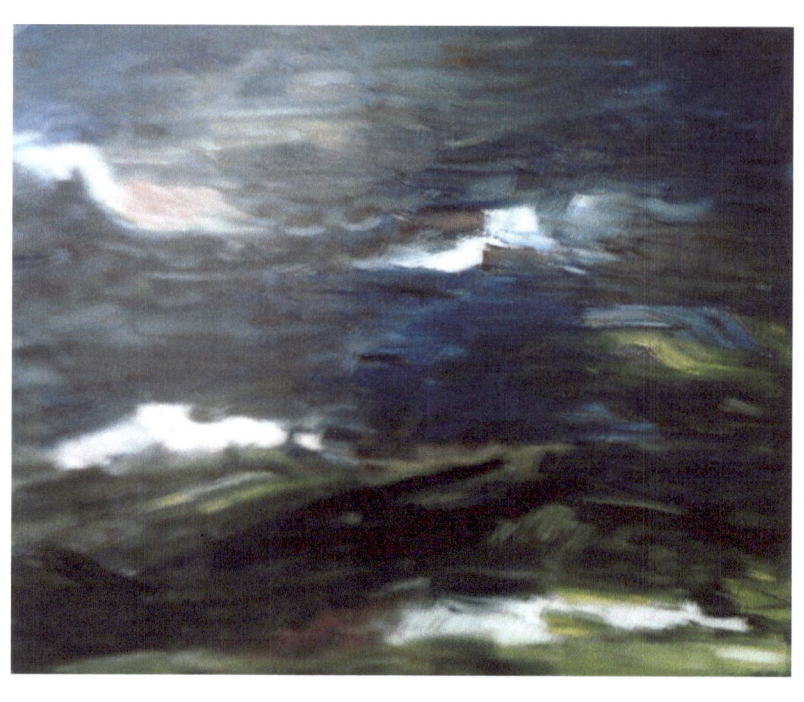

Street Art

 Although street art to most people means graffiti under bridges and on dirty walls. There is a feeling that the placing paintings on dry pavements is actually it. The suddenness of walking by a picture coupled with the amazement close up offers an offset a gap of redemption in someone's everyday belief. Many pass. A few photographed and on realises he can take it. And he does with an act of daring he has acquired something worth a few hundred pounds and the ironic thing is that he was meant to.

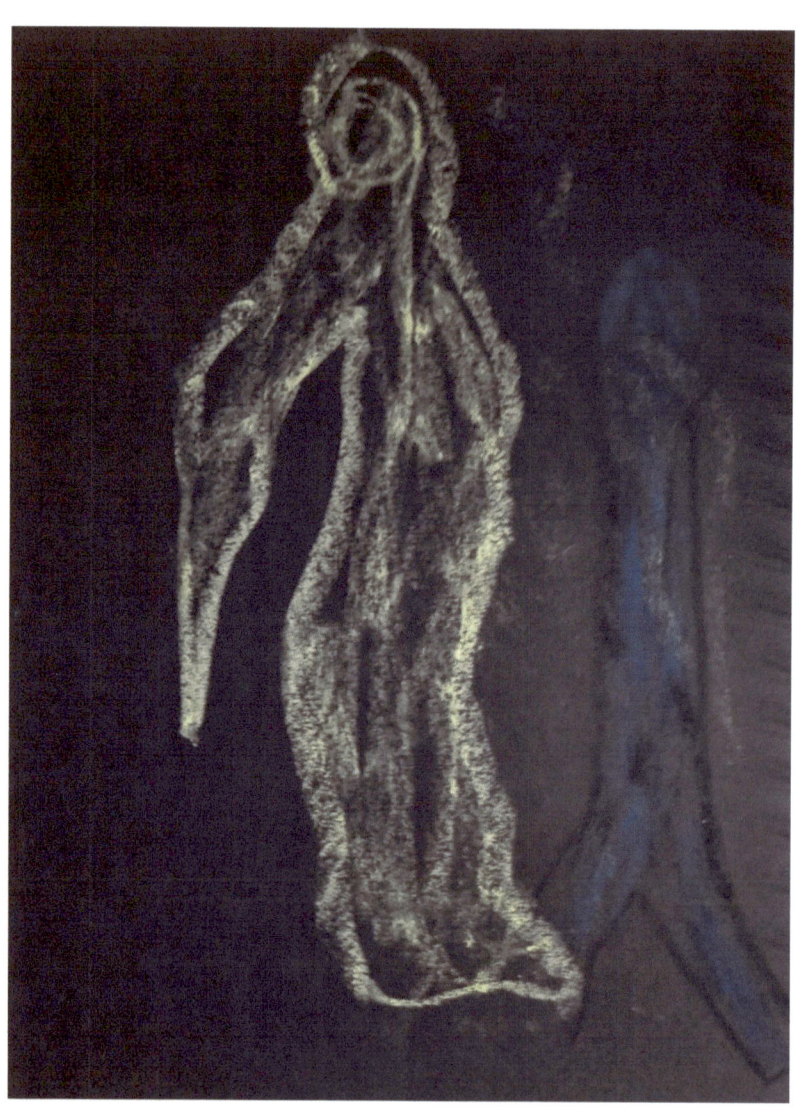

Lithographs

Originally lithographs were finished charcoal plates.Sturdy hard backed pieces inground black and white.They were Drawn across with palette knives and being solid they were like bank notes measure.
Today the art of it is less complicated.A good pad of paper with a good weight is used with a deft touch of charcoal quickly drawn features,smudges and detail.This all ends up in the piece which is then sprayed with fixative.
If the piece is true,it will remain the recurring and become a lithograph of the 21st century.

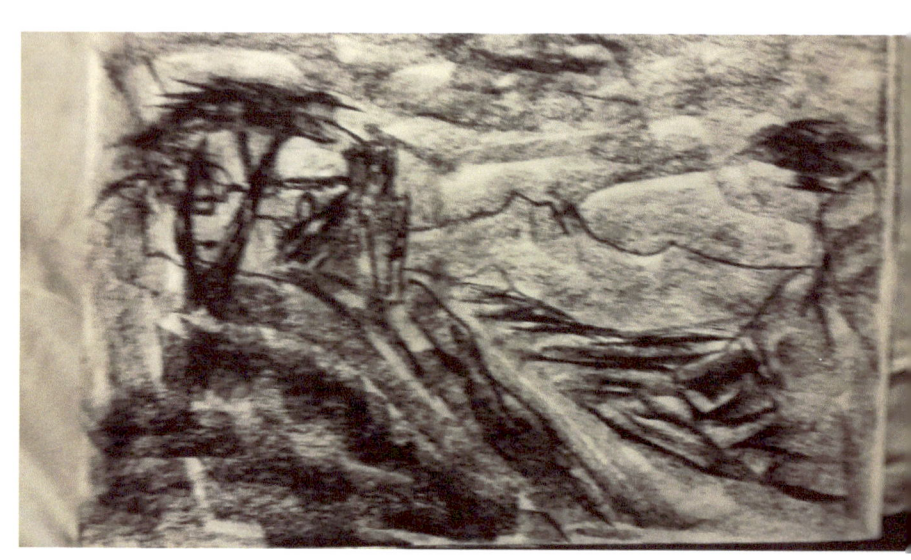

First melancholy

This is a state a mood to exist in which the participant in usually autumn and winter uses these profound emotions to channel through themselves the beauty or feeling of sadness onto canvas.As this is usually complex the feeling of being affected by things is to be sensible to the real and to be an artist.

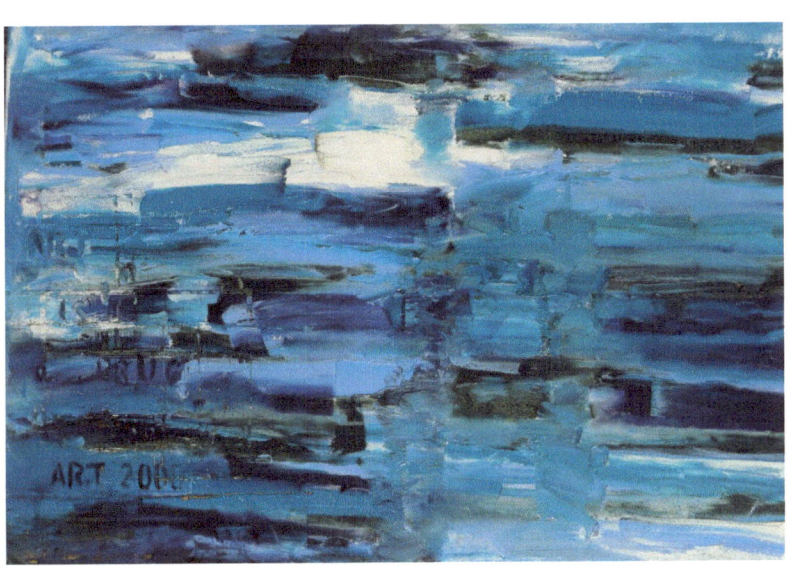

Futurism

Shapes colours angels and perspective.All these things were thrown in a different way to not show us the future but to construct it as the 20th century unfolded.Many show the world wars in their hard realities although not seeing these things in real life art was the truth which was hidden from us.Most of the art is now forgotten about but kept as a reminder of what things look like when it goes wrong.

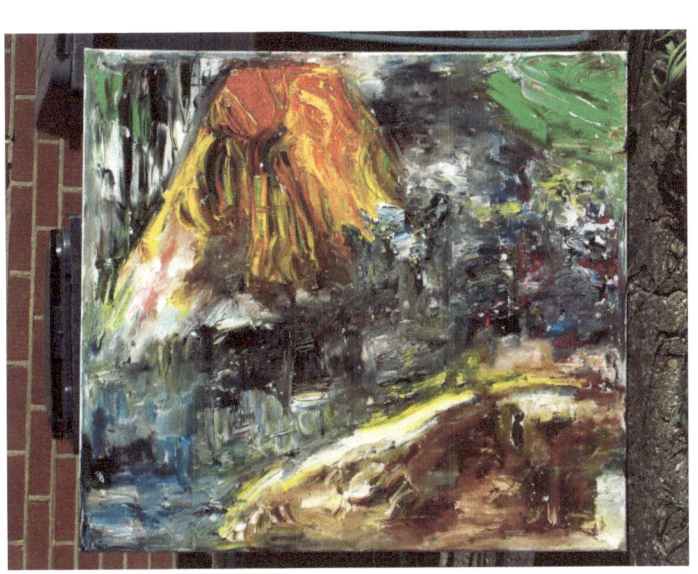

Romanticism

Romantiscism is the name of peoples beliefs that are drawn from nature from the divine creation.Many of the paintings are evening dusk and sunsets evoking the sense of mystery and love.There is a growing sense of going to the roots ,the natural,the beginning and in inheriting beauty from nature They live the life of spirit.

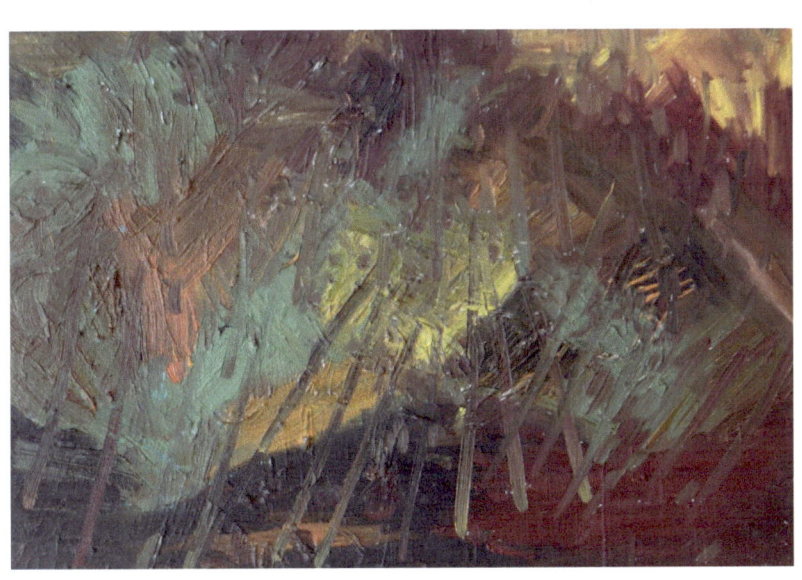

Master tradition

This is what is taught the guidelines to art the framework of which builds knowledge.This is from the pantheon of great painters who each have a technique which ensures proper imagination perspective flesh tone light shade and depth.Whereas a lot of art is not this and is a rebellion against this to achieve proper fine art is a must.To earn a decent living from art this paralellax to the masters is essential many believe to sell their paintings.However the artistic movements which became a recognised reality all disobeyed the rules.

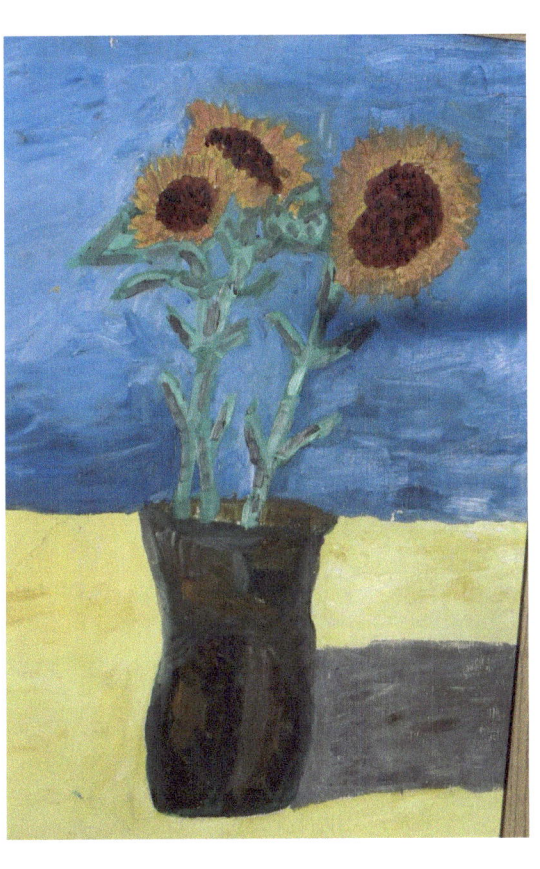

Charcoal

What could possibly conceive a type of rough half sketch and deep scope that charcoal drawings develop from.Of course the answer is imprisonment.For whatever reason this happens the best charcoals come out of adversity and despair rather than a love of art.So these are smuggled in and out of prisons and reach the hands of the ever watchful art collectors.

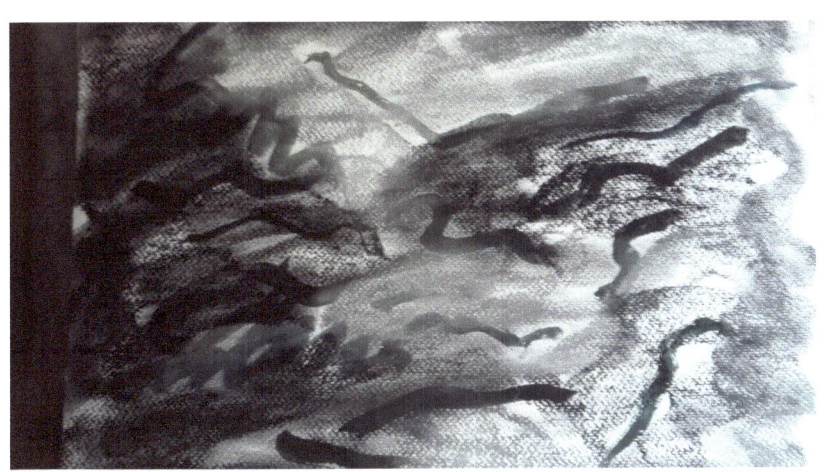

Kirchner

The antithesis of this is Ernst Ludwig Kirchner.Work during violence trying to escape it through pictures.An unlikely saviour to the German and world state of mind suffered so greatly for a beautiful mind.Everything was try destroy just him and his folky art.An architect of the German spirit,the hidden people the scenes he was much pressed to work impossibly hard.Sometimes at night while this gap lasted.The result twenty thousand pieces and a record of the German tradition.Eventually the hard work and drug use got the better of him and the world turned to war,he shot himself.

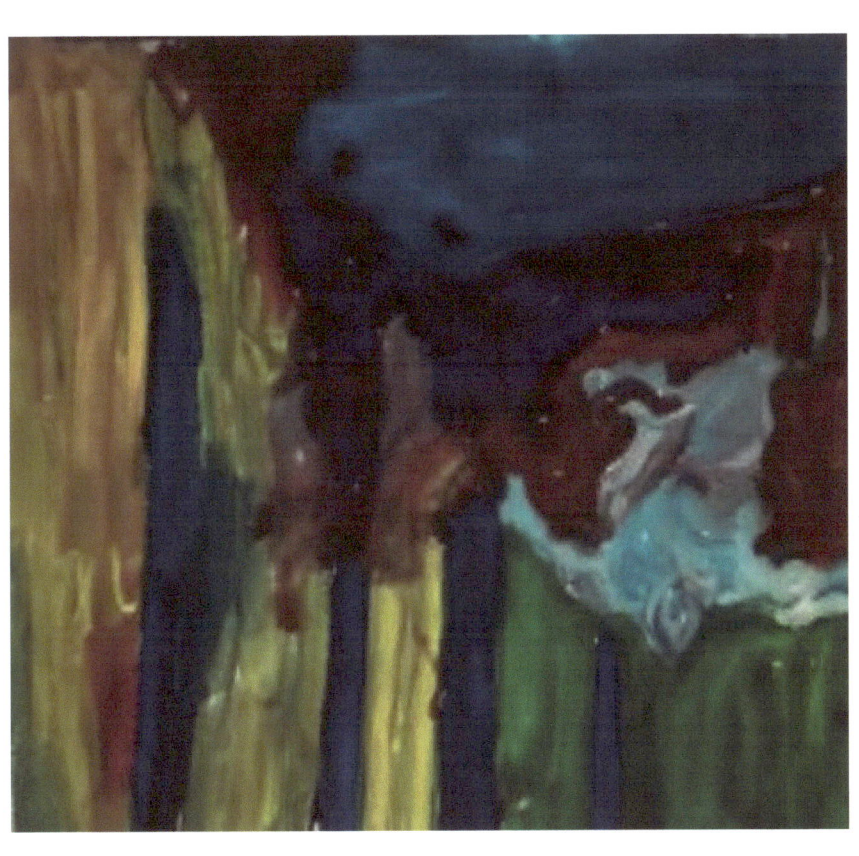

So the rudimentary of art has made a statement of belief an exploring of different meanings and is a mystery thought of.Painting is the profession of lost souls,the recording of a moment in time and at best a celestial connection.An expression of nostalgia learning to love again.

There are two sights to not lose.
i) Synethesiatic paintings which speak or make sounds.
ii) Metasynth a computer program which transforms sound into pictures.

www.ingramcontent.com/pod-product-compliance
Lightning Source LLC
Chambersburg PA
CBHW040300220526
45473CB00002B/543